Original title:
Solitude's Sonnet

Copyright © 2024 Creative Arts Management OÜ
All rights reserved.

Author: Julian Prescott
ISBN HARDBACK: 978-9916-90-732-0
ISBN PAPERBACK: 978-9916-90-733-7

Serene Whispers of the Night

Stars sprinkle dreams in the sky,
Moonlight dances, soft and shy.
Gentle breezes, secrets shared,
In the stillness, hearts laid bare.

Crickets sing their lullabies,
While the world in slumber lies.
Nature's hush, an embracing quilt,
Where tranquility finds no guilt.

Silhouettes in silver glow,
Whispered stories from below.
Each shadow tells a tale of old,
In the night, warmth unfolds.

Peaceful moments wrapped in grace,
Time slows down, a tender pace.
In the dark, our fears take flight,
We find solace in the night.

The Quiet Resilience

Through the storms, we stand so tall,
With gentle strength, we face it all.
Roots run deep, in earth we trust,
Rise again from ashes, dust.

Silent battles in the heart,
Crafting courage, playing the part.
With every trial, we learn to grow,
In the shadows, resilience glows.

Hands once trembling, now they fight,
Finding hope within the night.
With whispered dreams, we take our stand,
Building futures, hand in hand.

In the quiet, voices swell,
Strength in silence, breaking the shell.
Together we weave our woven fate,
In quiet resilience, we celebrate.

Portrait of a Lonely Heart

In the mirror, a shadow stares,
Silent cries from words unshared.
Loneliness, a delicate art,
Crafting echoes within the heart.

Brushstrokes of emotion blend,
Fragrant memories twist and bend.
Hues of longing paint the sky,
Yet in stillness, spirits fly.

Each glance tells a story untold,
A canvas with colors bold.
Yearnings carved in every line,
Time weaves solitude like wine.

In the whispers of the night,
Lonely hearts seek out the light.
A masterpiece of ache and grace,
Finding solace in one's embrace.

Chronicles of the Unheard

In the shadows, voices rest,
Stories buried, dreams suppressed.
Each heartbeat tells a tale forlorn,
In silence, vibrant worlds are born.

Echoes roam in crowded streets,
Words unspoken, life repeats.
Untold journeys yearn for light,
In the dark, they take their flight.

Wisps of thoughts like gentle rain,
Gather wisdom, cradle pain.
Chronicles weave through time and space,
In every whisper, we find grace.

Those unheard have much to say,
Hidden truths won't fade away.
In their tales, a love profound,
Waiting patiently to be found.

The Peace of Emptiness

In quiet moments, shadows play,
Where worries fade, and silence stays.
The heart finds rest, in gentle ease,
Embracing calm, like softest breeze.

Within the void, a whisper sings,
Of nothingness, the freedom brings.
A tranquil mind, no need for sound,
In emptiness, true peace is found.

Silent Stanzas

Words unspoken, softly felt,
In the quiet, emotions melt.
A gentle pause, a knowing glance,
In silence, life begins to dance.

Each heartbeat echoes, time stands still,
In hidden layers, dreams we fill.
Through silent stanzas, truth unfolds,
In hushed whispers, our story molds.

A Tapestry of One

Threads of color, interweave,
In every moment, we believe.
A single heart, a layered song,
Together, we are ever strong.

In the seams where stories blend,
Life's rich patterns stretch and bend.
A woven tale, with love entwined,
In this tapestry, peace we find.

Beneath the Stillness

Beneath the stillness, waters deep,
A world of secrets, hidden keep.
In gentle waves, the silence flows,
With every ripple, wisdom grows.

The heart, a vessel, calm and clear,
In tranquil depths, we shed our fear.
Beneath the stillness, we discover,
In quietude, we find each other.

Meditations in the Empty Chair

Silence fills the vacant space,
Thoughts gather with a gentle grace.
In the stillness, shadows play,
Echoes of the words we say.

Dust motes dance in light's embrace,
Memories linger, time's retrace.
The chair awaits with open arms,
A witness to our fleeting charms.

Within its frame, we find our peace,
Moments of the heart's release.
With each sigh, a breath anew,
In the quiet, we pursue.

So let the world outside forget,
In this stillness, we are met.
A space for dreams, a sacred pause,
In the chair, we find our cause.

A Solitary Astral Voyage

Beneath the stars, I drift afar,
A journey guided by a star.
Infinite whispers call my name,
In the dark, I feel the flame.

Galaxies spin, their colors bright,
In this vastness, I take flight.
Planets hum a distant tune,
Cradled by the silver moon.

Time dissolves in cosmic flow,
Among the nebulae, I glow.
In solitude, I find my home,
Across the void, I freely roam.

Every spark a story told,
In silence, the universe unfolds.
Lost and found in space's grace,
In the stillness, I embrace.

The Heart's Retreat

In the forest deep and wide,
Where shadows softly glide,
A whisper calls, a gentle breeze,
To rest beneath the ancient trees.

Among the roots, the secrets lie,
Wrapped in silence, where dreams fly,
Each heartbeat speaks, a tender sound,
In solitude, peace is found.

The brook hums low, a timeless tune,
Kissed by the light of the silver moon,
Here worries fade like morning mist,
In this haven, all is bliss.

Solace Beneath the Stars.

Under the velvet sky so vast,
Where moments linger, memories cast,
Stars above twinkle like a dream,
In silence whispers love's sweet theme.

A gentle night wraps all in peace,
As if the world is set to cease,
Every sigh a breath of grace,
In stillness, we find our place.

Beneath the cosmos, hearts unite,
In the glow of the soft moonlight,
Holding dreams, so close, so dear,
In the night, there's nothing to fear.

Whispers in the Quiet

When night descends and shadows creep,
The world around begins to sleep,
In the stillness, voices blend,
Each whisper carries, hearts to mend.

Softly spoken, secrets shared,
In every pause, we've truly cared,
The quiet holds a sacred space,
Where every tear can find its place.

A gentle nudge, a soft reply,
In whispers, dreams are set to fly,
With every word, a bond does form,
In the silence, hearts stay warm.

Echoes of a Silent Heart

A silent heart can speak so loud,
In quiet moments, feeling proud,
Every beat an echo true,
Resonates in shades of blue.

Through hushed sighs, it tells a tale,
Of love and loss that may prevail,
In capturing the fleeting time,
Each echo speaks a subtle rhyme.

In solitude, the heart resides,
With tender fears that it confides,
Within the stillness, strength is found,
In echoes soft, love's whispers sound.

Echoes in the Quiet

In the hush of nightfall's grace,
Soft shadows find their place.
Whispers float on the air,
Silent secrets everywhere.

Footsteps fade like distant dreams,
Wrapped in moonlight's silver beams.
Every heartbeat, a soft sigh,
Echoes linger as time slips by.

Stars above in twinkling dance,
Lost in thoughts, I find my chance.
To embrace the tranquil sound,
Where peace and stillness can be found.

In this realm where moments flow,
I meet the parts of me I know.
Echoes whisper, calm and bright,
In the gentle fold of night.

Whispers of the Alone

In corners where shadows play,
Thoughts drift, soft as the day.
Voices linger in the air,
Carried on a breeze so rare.

Moments captured, fears unfold,
Tales of solitude retold.
In this stillness, wisdom grows,
As the heart in silence knows.

Each breath a song of its own,
In the quiet, I have grown.
Whispers of the past align,
In the solitude, I find shine.

Finding strength in what is lost,
Learning well the hidden cost.
In the echoes, lessons dwell,
In every story, there's a spell.

Solitary Symphony

Strings of silence softly weave,
Crafting melodies that cleave.
Every note, a fleeting wisp,
Dancing on a quiet tryst.

In the stillness, instruments wait,
For the heart to orchestrate.
Fingers touch the strings anew,
Awakening the sound so true.

Rhythms pulse through the night air,
Creating art, stripped bare.
Each heartbeat, a steady drum,
In solitude, the notes will hum.

Daring once to dream alone,
In this symphony, I've grown.
Every silence, a chance to feel,
In the quiet, my soul can heal.

Embrace of the Empty

In the hollows of the space,
I find echoes of my grace.
Empty rooms, yet filled with light,
Casting shadows soft and bright.

Memories linger like a song,
Reminding me where I belong.
In the void, I hear the call,
Embracing everything and all.

Each breath expands the silent air,
Whispers dance without a care.
To be alone, to feel so whole,
In the empty, I find my soul.

With open arms, I greet the night,
Finding joy in the absence of fright.
In the embrace of what is bare,
I discover life and dare to care.

Solitary Reflections

In quiet corners where shadows play,
I find the echo of what was said.
Time slips softly, night turns to day,
A whisper of dreams, a thread unshed.

The mirror holds a gaze so deep,
It knows the secrets of my soul.
In silence, all my memories creep,
Their weight both heavy and making me whole.

A single step on an empty street,
The world moves on, yet I stand still.
In solitude, there's a bittersweet,
A moment caught, a fleeting thrill.

Here in the stillness, I reflect,
Finding beauty in the quiet strife.
The heart learns to gently connect,
With every breath, I claim my life.

Traces of an Elusive Presence

In the spaces where shadows dance,
I feel a stir, a gentle sigh.
A fleeting glance, a soft romance,
An echo whispers, 'You did try.'

Lost in the corridors of thought,
Your laughter lingers in the air.
In memories, solace is sought,
Yet every dream leads me to despair.

A scent that wafts on evening mist,
Reminds me of the times we shared.
Each moment feels like a lost tryst,
With every glance, love declared.

The presence fades, but still it stays,
A trace of you, both near and far.
In quiet nights, I count the days,
With every wish on a distant star.

Harmony in Absence

In quietude, I find my song,
A melody woven, soft and clear.
Though you're away, I feel so strong,
The notes remain, they hold you near.

Each silence gives a room to breathe,
Where echoes of your laughter lie.
They weave a quilt, no need to grieve,
For love transcends the how and why.

In spaces left by joy's retreat,
There blooms a garden, rich and wild.
With every heartbeat, life feels sweet,
A rhythm found in absence styled.

So here I stand, embracing calm,
With hope that carries me along.
In harmony, I weave a balm,
A soothing tune, our shared lifelong.

Waking Dreams of the Alone

In waking hours, my thoughts do roam,
Through landscapes born of twilight's glow.
The dreamt sensations feel like home,
Where lonely hearts can learn to flow.

Each morning brings a brand new start,
Yet shadows cling, familiar friends.
They whisper softly to my heart,
In solitude, the journey bends.

The dreams I chase through silent skies,
Illuminate the path I seek.
In every breath, a longing lies,
A promise whispered, soft and meek.

Awake or dream, the lines are blurred,
As I wander through realms unknown.
In every sigh, a wish deferred,
Waking dreams weave the fabric alone.

Imagined Conversations

In shadows of a whispered night,
Thoughts collide in silent flight.
Voices echo, soft and clear,
Words unspoken linger near.

Dreams weave tales of distant shores,
Carried by the wind's soft roars.
Each intonation, subtle grace,
A dance of souls in boundless space.

Time unfurls in tender sighs,
As flickering stars light up the skies.
Imagined meetings, hearts that blend,
In the corridors where thoughts ascend.

Moments captured, fleeting glow,
In this realm, where secrets flow.
Through the veil, we find a way,
In conversations, souls can stay.

The Silent Sanctuary

In nature's heart, a haven lies,
Where every whisper softly sighs.
The trees stand tall, a watchful crowd,
Embracing peace beneath their shroud.

Sunlight dances on the stream,
Casting shadows in a dream.
Gentle breezes cradle the air,
In this refuge, free of care.

With every step on mossy ground,
A tranquil pulse is all around.
Here, solitude invites the mind,
To seek the solace that's defined.

A heart at home, a spirit free,
In silence finds its melody.
In sanctuary, breaths align,
Unraveling the sacred sign.

Reflections in Solitary Waters

Glimmers dance on stillness deep,
Where secrets hide and shadows creep.
In turquoise pools, the sky's embrace,
Mirrors echo nature's grace.

Each ripple tells a story slow,
Of journeys taken long ago.
In silence speaks the past, profound,
As echoes of our thoughts resound.

The moonlight paints a silver hue,
On waters calm, so clear and true.
In solitude, reflections swirl,
As heartbeats tether, thoughts unfurl.

To seek the depths where silence lies,
In liquid truth beneath the skies.
In each drop, a world awaits,
Where time dissolves and fate creates.

A Journey Within Walls

Worn stones cradle whispered dreams,
Echoes linger in silent beams.
Through corridors of fading light,
Memories weave with deep insight.

Footsteps trace a timeless flow,
Where shadows dance and spirits glow.
Walls hold stories, secrets rare,
In quiet corners, love laid bare.

Each brick a keeper of the past,
Time's embrace will ever last.
The journey winds, yet feels so near,
In every creak, a voice we hear.

As darkness falls, the heart takes flight,
In walls of old, there shines a light.
A journey deep, both brave and kind,
Within these walls, we seek, we find.

The Echo of Longing

In the quiet of the night,
Whispers dance on gentle breeze,
Chasing shadows out of sight,
Filling hearts with silent pleas.

Stars above, a distant glow,
Each a wish from those who yearn,
In the stillness, feelings flow,
Echoes of a love we learn.

Time stands still, the world seems bare,
Memories linger, bittersweet,
In the silence, dreams laid bare,
Longing's touch is bittersweet.

Yet within this aching void,
Hope emerges like the dawn,
In the dark, love is employed,
With each echo, life moves on.

Solitary Serenade

Underneath the moon's soft light,
A lone figure starts to sing,
Notes that float into the night,
Hope and sorrow intertwining.

Empty streets beneath the stars,
Melodies of dreams untold,
Each refrain, a mark of scars,
Tales of warmth and hearts so bold.

Echoes of a past embrace,
Whispers lost in evening air,
In the silence, find a place,
Where the soul can shed its care.

Solitude, a friend so dear,
In its arms, the heart can mend,
Every note, a crystal clear,
Solitary serenade to send.

An Ode to the Unaccompanied

In the quiet of the morn,
Footsteps tread on paths unknown,
Each breath, a tale reborn,
A journey taken all alone.

The heart beats a steady drum,
Rhythms of a life unshared,
Seeking joy, feeling the numb,
In the stillness, yet prepared.

Stars may shine, but none beside,
Yet the spirit learns to soar,
Finding strength in every stride,
Ode to those who seek for more.

Though the world may seem so vast,
Every step is worth the fight,
In the soul, the shadows cast,
A light ignites within the night.

Tides of Tranquility

Waves cascade on golden shore,
Whispers of the ocean's peace,
In the calm, hearts start to soar,
Each new breath brings sweet release.

Moonlit paths on endless seas,
Guiding dreams towards the light,
With each ripple, moments freeze,
Swaying gently, pure delight.

Nature sings a lullaby,
Sands embrace the setting sun,
In this space where worries die,
Tides of calm, our hearts have won.

Flowing freely, let love lead,
Through the currents of our days,
In tranquility, we heed,
Life's soft whispers, gentle ways.

Musings of the Moonlit

Beneath the silver glow of night,
Whispers dance in soft delight.
Stars like diamonds softly gleam,
Carrying dreams within a dream.

Winds that twirl the ancient trees,
Sing of secrets, dark with ease.
The world pauses, time stands still,
Heartbeats echo, soft and shrill.

Shadows blend with light's embrace,
In this tranquil, sacred space.
Every sigh, a lover's plea,
As the moonlight cradles me.

Thoughts drift like clouds upon the tide,
In this magic, I confide.
With each glimmer, I find my way,
Musings linger, night turns day.

Confessions in the Dark

In the silence where shadows blend,
I reveal what I cannot send.
Secrets linger on whispered breath,
In the dark, we confront our death.

Heartbeats thud in unwritten tales,
Voices echo where trust prevails.
In hidden corners, truth takes flight,
Confessions linger in the night.

Fears laid bare like scars on skin,
Vows unspoken, where to begin?
Underneath the starlit gaze,
We offer souls in silent praise.

Hopes entwined with tangled dreams,
In shadows' grasp, nothing seems.
Yet in the dark, we find our spark,
Lighting paths, despite the stark.

Solitary Stanzas

In solitude, the heart takes flight,
Words cascade like stars at night.
Each stanza penned in quiet grace,
Crafts a world I can embrace.

Thoughts unravel, threads of gold,
Stories whisper, brave and bold.
With every line, I weave my fears,
Holding joy amidst the tears.

The paper knows my hidden dreams,
Ink flows freely, life redeems.
Solitary moments fill the page,
Poetry spirals, free from cage.

In silence, I find solace deep,
While distant echoes gently sweep.
Solitary stanzas, mine to keep,
In every word, my heart will leap.

Reflections of a Wandering Thought

Thoughts drift lightly on the breeze,
Like whispers lost among the trees.
Each reflection, a glimpse of light,
Guiding me through shades of night.

In the stillness, truth takes form,
A gentle voice amidst the storm.
Reflections ripple in quiet pools,
Shining wisdom, the heart's own jewels.

Wandering thoughts, they ebb and flow,
Through the landscapes, soft and slow.
With every pause, a chance to see,
The beauty in the fleeting free.

Through the corridors of my mind,
A tapestry of dreams entwined.
Reflections linger, softly caught,
In the depths of wandering thought.

Melodies of Melancholy

Soft whispers float through the night,
Carrying dreams out of sight.
A tune plays where shadows dwell,
In the silence, there's a spell.

Each note drips like falling rain,
A reminder of hidden pain.
Lingering in the fading light,
Melodies chase away the night.

Secrets sigh in distant air,
Hopes entwined in deep despair.
Notes of sorrow, pure and deep,
In the darkness, lost souls weep.

Under stars, they dance alone,
Hearts that ache, but never moan.
In the stillness, a voice calls,
Echoing through empty halls.

The Solitary Waltz

In a room where shadows play,
An empty chair, night turns to day.
A gentle sweep, a slow embrace,
Loneliness finds its rightful place.

Feet that glide on polished floor,
Echoes of laughter, now no more.
Silent partners in waltz of dreams,
Moving softly, lost in seams.

Reflections dance on walls so bare,
Whispers soft, float in the air.
Time stands still in quiet grace,
A heart aches in the empty space.

Each step taken, a fleeting glance,
Yearning for a forgotten dance.
Yet in solitude, we find our way,
Lost in night, alive in day.

Echoes of an Abandoned Heart

Once a flame, now merely ash,
A love that faded in a flash.
Whispers linger where you stood,
Promises lost in the quiet wood.

The shadows stretch, the night draws near,
Every echo sings of fear.
Words unspoken float on breeze,
Fragments of what used to please.

Each heartbeat a haunting sound,
In the silence, sorrow found.
Lonely rhythms, soft and stark,
The melody of a broken heart.

Yet hope hangs on the twilight air,
A memory, tender and rare.
In this stillness, dreams depart,
Leaving echoes of an abandoned heart.

Nocturne of the Isolated

Underneath a silver sky,
Lonely stars begin to cry.
In the night, shadows arise,
Whispers lost in soft goodbyes.

Moonlight dances on the ground,
Faintest heartbeat, barely found.
In the silence, solitude swirls,
A canvas where longing unfurls.

Softly played on broken strings,
A song of sorrow, what it brings.
Each note stings like morning dew,
A nocturne felt, but never knew.

In this world, so far apart,
Music weaves through every heart.
The isolated find their muse,
In the dark, they softly choose.

Lonesome Ballad

In the night when shadows creep,
A lonely heart begins to weep.
Whispers of the lost echo,
Where dreams and memories often flow.

Stars above seem far away,
Guiding tears that long to stay.
A song of sorrow fills the air,
As solitude becomes a prayer.

Each note a tale of pain and strife,
The melody reflects a life.
In silence echoes love's sweet ache,
A lonesome ballad, never fake.

Yet hope ignites the darkest skies,
A fragile flame that never dies.
Through every verse, a glimmer gleams,
As the heart embraces its own dreams.

The Silent Serenade

Beneath the moon's soft silver glow,
Whispers dance in breezes slow.
Nature sings a tune so sweet,
A silent serenade, a heartbeat.

Glimmers of twilight grace the land,
The stars like notes, so close at hand.
In stillness, harmony prevails,
As night unfolds its secret tales.

The world around, in quiet bliss,
Moments fleeting, sealed with a kiss.
In every pause, a story lies,
A serenade beneath the skies.

In shadows deep and dreams untold,
Whispers of the night unfold.
A silent song, forever true,
Awakens hope in hearts anew.

Reflections in Stillness

On tranquil lakes, the stars do rest,
Mirroring dreams that feel the best.
In stillness, thoughts begin to flow,
Reflections whisper what they know.

The calm unfolds in shades of night,
A gentle peace, an inner light.
With every ripple, secrets shared,
In quiet moments, hearts are bared.

Nature holds its breath in awe,
Each glance reveals what we once saw.
In stillness, wisdom calls our name,
Reflections spark a brighter flame.

The world, a canvas, softly glows,
In silence, contemplation grows.
As twilight dreams in whispers blend,
Reflections lead us to transcend.

Harmonies of the Hidden

In shadows deep, where silence dwells,
Mysteries whispered in secret spells.
Voices rise in subtle tone,
Harmonies of the hidden, alone.

Through the veil, where few have tread,
Echoes of heartbeats softly spread.
A symphony of life concealed,
In quiet moments, truths revealed.

Breath of nature, soft and low,
In every corner, feelings flow.
The unheard notes weave through the air,
Harmonies linger, rich and rare.

Awake the soul to listen close,
In hidden places, love can rose.
Each chord a journey yet unknown,
Harmonies whisper, we are not alone.

Fragments of Solitary Days

In a quiet room, shadows play,
Worn pages turn, in light's soft sway.
Memories linger, whispers of grace,
Each moment etched, time can't erase.

Faded photographs, smiles in frames,
Echoes of laughter, flickering flames.
Loneliness wraps like a gentle shroud,
In solace found, away from the crowd.

Drops of rain on a window glass,
Nature's heartbeat, a quiet pass.
Moments unfold like petals of time,
In solitude's song, I find my rhyme.

As dusk descends, the world holds its breath,
In stillness, I ponder the dance of death.
Fragments of days, both bitter and sweet,
In solitude's arms, my heart finds its beat.

The Unseen Horizons

Barefoot on paths where shadows dwell,
Chasing the dreams that I can't quite tell.
A whisper calls from the edge of night,
Guiding my heart towards distant light.

Mountains rise high, cloaked in the mist,
Secrets of worlds that I long to twist.
Each step I take, the vastness unfolds,
Stories of lands that the heart still holds.

Stars above twinkle in silent grace,
Hidden horizons where hopes interlace.
In the quiet, I find the embrace,
Of journeys begun, in time's gentle chase.

The sky's hue shifts as dawn breaks anew,
Unseen horizons present their view.
With every breath, I long to explore,
The vast unknown that forever beckons more.

Still Waters Run Deep

In a tranquil pond, reflections lie,
Beneath the surface, silent thoughts sigh.
The world above, a fleeting glance,
Yet depths hold tales of fate and chance.

Gentle ripples, a soft serenade,
Whispers of secrets in quiet shade.
Nature's breath, in hushed refrain,
In stillness, echoes of joy and pain.

Every pebble a story to share,
In liquid mirrors, emotions laid bare.
Time drifts slowly in this calm keep,
Where still waters run deep, and dreams leap.

As twilight falls, colors profoundly sweep,
In the hush of night, my soul takes a leap.
Embracing the depths where shadows entwine,
In the heart of still waters, I find what's mine.

The Cloak of Quietude

Wrapped in silence like a soft embrace,
The world slows down, finding its place.
Gentle whispers weave through the air,
In the cloak of quietude, a sacred prayer.

Hidden from chaos that sings its loud tune,
Moments of peace, under the watchful moon.
Softly I wander, heart open wide,
In the depths of stillness, I find my guide.

The rustling leaves, a lullaby sweet,
Nature's rhythm, my heart skips a beat.
Lost in a reverie, time ceases to flow,
In the cloak of quietude, my spirit can grow.

Beneath the stars, I gather my dreams,
In the soft glimmers, the universe gleams.
In solitude's hold, I discover my soul,
In the cloak of quietude, I become whole.

Dreamscape of the Alone

In twilight's gentle embrace, I roam,
Wishing to find a place called home.
Stars whisper secrets in the night,
Guiding lost souls toward the light.

Echoes of laughter ripple through dreams,
Fleeting moments, or so it seems.
Chasing shadows, I wander deep,
In night's cradle, I silently weep.

Mountains rise like obstacles high,
Underneath the vast, endless sky.
Yet hope flickers within my chest,
A flicker that never lets me rest.

In solitude's arms, I find my grace,
Learning to dance in this empty space.
Dreamscape painted in hues of blue,
A masterpiece waiting to unveil its view.

The Whistle of the Wind

A soft lullaby, the breeze sings low,
Through the trees, it weaves a flow.
Branches sway like dancers chic,
Revealing secrets that lips dare not speak.

Clouds drift lazily across the sky,
Each one a canvas, passing by.
Nature's chorus, a rhythmic sigh,
Echoing dreams that never die.

The whistle beckons, a siren's call,
Gently urging me to rise and fall.
In its arms, worries seem to fade,
With every note, a new serenade.

Fingers brush against the sky's veil,
With whispers of stories carried in the gale.
In the union of air and sound,
An invisible spirit can always be found.

In the Absence of Noise

Silence blankets the restless night,
In its arms, I find respite.
Thoughts unravel with every breath,
In quietude, I brush with death.

Time slows down, a steady beat,
In this stillness, my heart finds heat.
Moments expand, horizons wide,
Lost in the ebb of the rising tide.

The pause between the heart's demands,
Where dreams entwine with gentle hands.
Whispers float upon the air's seam,
In absence, I am free to dream.

Every tick of the clock is a sigh,
In the shadows where memories lie.
In the silence, I reclaim my voice,
In the stillness, I make my choice.

Shadows of the Mind

Fleeting flashes of thought arise,
Dancing timidly in the dark skies.
Threads of memory, tightly spun,
In the tapestry of what's undone.

Haunting whispers float in the air,
Echoes of dreams woven with despair.
Stillness reigns where chaos once thrived,
Shadows linger, silently deprived.

Images flicker, edges blurred,
In corners of the mind, thoughts stirred.
A restless quest for the light of day,
As shadows compete in the mind's ballet.

Yet in their depths, a spark ignites,
Guiding lost souls to hidden heights.
In shadows, hope begins to climb,
Transforming fear into rhythm and rhyme.

In Search of Still Waters

In the hush of dawn's embrace,
Reflections dance on gentle streams.
Nature whispers soft and low,
In search of peace, we trace our dreams.

Beneath the boughs where shadows play,
The world outside begins to fade.
Time slows down, a subtle sway,
In stillness, hearts are unafraid.

Each ripple holds a secret tale,
Carried forth by tender winds.
A tranquil path where hopes set sail,
In search of strength that nature lends.

Here in the calm, we find our ground,
The weight of worry drifts away.
In unity with silence found,
Our souls can breathe, our spirits sway.

The Unvoiced Desires

In shadows deep, where wishes dwell,
A heart beats loud, but lips stay sealed.
What dreams reside and yearn to swell,
In silence, pain is often healed.

Through crowded rooms, the glance can weave,
A tapestry of thoughts unspun.
What truths we hide, what we believe,
A battle fought, yet never won.

With every heartbeat, whispers flow,
In secret sighs, the longing grows.
Each unvoiced wish, a silent throe,
In aching depths, our courage shows.

In time, the soul may find its voice,
Unraveling the threads of night.
With every pulse, we make the choice,
To share our truth and seek the light.

The Lantern of Isolation

Amidst the dark, a lantern glows,
A fragile light in endless night.
It flickers soft, the solace grows,
In solitude, the heart takes flight.

Each beam a story, every shade,
Reflects the whispers of the past.
In quiet moments, fears cascade,
As shadows dance, memories cast.

The world outside may roar and sway,
Yet here within, the fire's warm.
In isolation's gentle sway,
We find a sense of calm, a form.

So let the lantern guide the way,
Through winding paths and endless tales.
In solitude, we learn to stay,
And nurture strength when silence prevails.

A Portrait of Quiet Courage

In stillness rests a burning flame,
A heart steadfast, a spirit bold.
In whispers soft, they stake their claim,
Each challenge faced, a tale retold.

Among the storms, they stand alone,
With silent strength that few can see.
A courage drawn from deep unknown,
In every choice, they set them free.

With patience woven through their days,
They navigate the winding roads.
Each step a brush, each thought a praise,
In quietude, their spirit glows.

A portrait framed by trials faced,
In hues of grace, resilience shown.
With every breath, their truth embraced,
A testament that they've outgrown.

A Symphony of Shadows

In twilight's embrace, whispers roam,
Dancing with shadows, far from home.
Echoes of silence, a soft refrain,
Melodies linger, a haunting pain.

Beneath the moon's watchful, silver eye,
Shadows enchant where dark secrets lie.
A symphony sings in the cool night air,
The heart finds solace, though none might care.

Winds carry stories of days long past,
Each note we weave, a spell to last.
In the depth of shadows, beauty unfurls,
Life intertwines in its mystic swirls.

Together we weave, a fabric of night,
Holding our dreams in the dimming light.
A tale of shadows, a chorus so deep,
In silence we gather, our secrets to keep.

The Lament of Stillness

In the hush of dawn, where moments wait,
Time flows slowly, a heavy weight.
Cries of the heart, unheard, unsaid,
A symphony lies in the dreams we dread.

Echoes of laughter fade with the light,
Fleeting memories dance, vanish from sight.
Beneath the still surface, storms gently brew,
A landscape of longing, painted in blue.

Where silence reigns, shadows oft dwell,
Each breath a story, a tale to tell.
In corners of quiet, some truth must hide,
As the world turns softly, we turn inside.

The lament of stillness, a voice of grace,
Longing and hoping in this sacred space.
Though the world rushes on, we pause and see,
In echoes of quiet, we find our plea.

Yearning in the Void

In the depths of night, when dreams unfold,
A yearning stirs, fierce and bold.
Lost in the ether, we search for light,
In the vastness of silence, we find our fight.

Thoughts drift like shadows, aimless and clear,
Longing for something, an echo we hear.
Stars whisper secrets, the darkness implores,
In the void of yearning, our spirit soars.

Time stretches gently, a fragile thread,
Between the wanting and paths we tread.
Yet still we wander, through silence we roam,
In the heart of the void, we seek a home.

A dance of desires, a fragile ballet,
In the yearning silence, we choose to stay.
For in the void, our hopes take flight,
A spark in the darkness, a flicker of light.

Breath of the Unseen

In the quiet moments, the unseen breath,
Whispers of life, a dance with death.
Each sigh a promise, a fleeting chance,
In the silent spaces, we find our dance.

Ghosts of the past gently brush our skin,
Echoes remind us, they're never thin.
In twilight's embrace, shadows entwine,
The breath of the unseen, our hearts align.

Wisps of the morning, soft as a sigh,
Linger like dreams as they pass by.
In the depth of silence, we learn to hear,
The breath of the unseen, always near.

Together we weave, this fragile thread,
With each whispered secret, our spirits wed.
In the bloom of the night, when time stands still,
The breath of the unseen, our hearts fulfill.

The Lonesome Bard's Tune

In shadows deep, the bard does sigh,
His melodies drift, like whispers nigh.
A heart once full, now echoes bare,
Strumming strings in the chill of air.

Each note a tear, a silent plea,
In faded lights, lost harmony.
With every chord, a memory plays,
Of laughter bright in sunlit days.

The moon above, a silver guide,
While time rolls on, the moments slide.
A solitary song unfolds,
Tales of love that the night enfolds.

Yet through the night, a spark remains,
Hope in his heart, through joy and pains.
With every strum, he finds his way,
The lonesome bard will sing today.

Reverie of an Isolated Mind

In quiet corners, thoughts take flight,
A dance of dreams in the pale moonlight.
Memories weave a tapestry bright,
Yet solitude grips, a lingering fright.

Whispers of time echo so far,
In silence deep, like a distant star.
Visions drift on a tranquil stream,
Walls close in, stifling the dream.

Each notion spins in an endless round,
Querying truths that still confound.
The chambers echo, the shadows blend,
Seeking comfort where thoughts ascend.

In this refuge, both sweet and grim,
A mind finds solace, a fragile hymn.
Though isolated, a heart can soar,
For reverie's dance opens the door.

Embrace of the Empty Room

Four walls stand firm, an echoing sound,
In this empty room, stillness is found.
Dust motes dance in the soft sunlight,
Whispers of past dreams take flight.

A chair sits lonely, a table bare,
Memories linger, still hanging there.
Faded laughter, shadows of grace,
The warmth of presence now leaves no trace.

In silence deep, the heart learns to hear,
The softest calls of what once was dear.
Embraced by void, it wraps so tight,
Yet within the stillness, there shines a light.

The empty room speaks in gentle tones,
Cradling the soul, the paraffin moans.
Though solitude reigns where dreams once bloomed,
In the stillness found, new hope is groomed.

Starlit Solitude

Beneath the stars, the night unfolds,
In whispered tales, the universe molds.
Glimmers of light, a cosmic embrace,
In starlit solitude, I find my place.

The vast expanse calls with a gentle grace,
Each pinprick glows, a familiar face.
Dreams are woven in threads of night,
Solace discovered in quiet flight.

Here in the dark, the heart can roam,
Finding its way, it feels like home.
The silence sings a soothing song,
In starlit solitude, I belong.

With every blink, the heavens wink,
As thoughts cascade, I pause to think.
In the embrace of the night's array,
Starlit solitude leads me away.

A Memory of One

In a gentle breeze, whispers call,
Echoes of laughter, soft and small.
A glance, a spark, a fleeting trace,
In shadows of time, we find our place.

Moments cherished, tucked away,
Fading like dusk at the end of the day.
Fragments of joy, stitched with care,
A single heartbeat, forever there.

Time dances on, yet still it clings,
To every story that memory sings.
In depths of silence, memories reside,
A tapestry woven, where love abides.

Through fading light, we find our way,
In the warmth of dreams that softly sway.
A memory of one, forever bright,
In the chambers of dusk, a guiding light.

Heart of the Quiet Woods

In the heart of woods, where shadows play,
   Whispers of nature greet the day.
  Leaves in the stillness dance and sway,
    Guarding secrets, come what may.

Moss carpets paths where footsteps tread,
   Ancient trees hold the stories read.
  A silence profound, a sacred space,
    In every corner, a gentle grace.

Birds sing softly, their melodies true,
  Echoing dreams, both old and new.
Sunlight spills through the leafy crown,
  In the quiet woods, I lay me down.

Here in the still, my spirit roams free,
  The heart of the woods, a sanctuary.
  Nature listens, in beauty I trust,
    In the quiet, I find my must.

Soliloquy of the Soul

In the depth of night, my thoughts take flight,
A soliloquy whispered, soft and light.
Reflections weave through shadow's embrace,
I stand alone, a stranger's face.

Questions linger in the still of air,
What does it mean to truly care?
In the silence, wisdom unfolds,
A tapestry rich, in stories told.

Through the darkest hours, I seek the flame,
A flicker of hope, calling my name.
Each heartbeat echoes, a rhythm sincere,
In the soliloquy, I hold what's dear.

A dance of thoughts, a chorus of dreams,
In the solitude, the soul redeems.
From the depths, I rise and confess,
In the silence, my soul finds rest.

Stars Above Empty Spaces

In the vast expanse, stars brightly gleam,
Whispers of wishes, caught in a dream.
Spaces unfilled, yet alive with grace,
Each twinkling light, a timeless embrace.

The universe spins in a cosmic dance,
A tapestry woven, a happenstance.
Echoes of stories from ages past,
In the starlit skies, forever cast.

Lonely hearts gaze, seeking a sign,
Lost in the void, yet hoping to shine.
Together we yearn for a piece of the light,
In the empty spaces, we find our fight.

Above us, the stars weave tales untold,
In the night's embrace, our dreams unfold.
In celestial whispers, we find our place,
Stars above us, fill the empty space.

Ballad of the Forsaken

In the twilight's fading glow,
A whisper lingers low,
Shadows dance with silent grief,
Lost souls seek a brief relief.

Wandering through the empty streets,
Echoes of forgotten beats,
Promises left unspoken,
Hearts that lie cold and broken.

Beneath the stars, a tale unfolds,
Of love that's lost, of dreams untold,
Each tear a droplet in the night,
A ballad sung from endless plight.

Yet, hope may flicker, soft and pale,
In the depths of this darkened tale,
For even in despair's fast grip,
A glimmer waits for the heart's quick trip.

The Lonely Canvas

Upon the canvas, shades reside,
Each stroke a story, deep inside,
Colors blend but lack a voice,
In quiet hues, there is no choice.

The painter's brush, unsteady hand,
Creates a world that can't withstand,
Loneliness in every line,
An essence trapped, devoid of time.

Yet in the emptiness, a spark,
A tinge of hope breaks through the dark,
A whispered dream, a fleeting light,
In solitude, comes forth the fight.

And in this stillness, creation flows,
From heart to art, a love that grows,
For though alone, the colors sing,
A symphony that pain can bring.

Enigma of the Quiet Mind

In silent chambers, thoughts collide,
Whispers echo, nowhere to hide,
A labyrinth of shadows deep,
Where secrets dwell and silence weeps.

The quiet mind, a puzzle vast,
Chasing echoes of the past,
Fragments scattered, lost in time,
Illusions weave a cryptic rhyme.

Yet in this maze, a truth unveils,
Amidst the fog, the spirit sails,
Through stillness, clarity is born,
From tangled webs, the heart is sworn.

So journey forth through shadows cast,
Embrace the silence, hold it fast,
For in the quiet, wisdom glows,
A hidden path where knowing flows.

Solace in the Shadows

Beneath the veil of night so deep,
Where secrets dwell and silence keep,
A haven found in darkened folds,
Solace whispered, comfort unfolds.

In shadows cast by flickering light,
Hearts entwined in the depths of night,
Each sigh a balm for weary souls,
A refuge where the spirit consoles.

From pain's embrace, sweet solace springs,
A gentle hush that softly sings,
In every corner, solace stays,
A flicker of hope that gently sways.

So wander here, where shadows blend,
In quietude, let your heart mend,
For in embrace of night so warm,
You'll find your strength, the softest charm.

Reverie of the Unseen

In twilight's embrace, whispers gleam,
A world unfolds, beyond the seam.
Stars weave tales, the night bestows,
Secrets held in twilight's throes.

Gentle echoes dance on air,
Fleeting visions, light as prayer.
Through the mist, lost dreams appear,
A canvas drawn, so crystal clear.

In shadows deep, where silence lies,
The heart can see with open eyes.
A reverie stirs, unbound and free,
In the unseen, we cease to be.

A specter's sigh, a timeless song,
In knowing hearts, we all belong.
Together lost, together found,
In reverie's clasp, forever bound.

The Quietude Chronicles

In corners soft where whispers dwell,
A soothing watch, a silent spell.
The world outside, a distant hum,
In quietude, our souls succumb.

Beneath the boughs, where shadows rest,
Peaceful moments feel the best.
Each breath a balm, each pause a tune,
In stillness wrapped beneath the moon.

The clock's soft tick, a gentle guide,
As heartbeats sync with time's slow ride.
Through tranquil paths, the mind can roam,
In chronicles of quiet, we find home.

Close your eyes and drift away,
To places where the spirits play.
In every breath, truth intertwines,
In quietude, the heart defines.

Shadows of One

A solitary path I tread,
In shadows cast, where dreams are led.
Each step a tale, each glance a spark,
In solitude, I find my mark.

Embracing dusk, the silence sings,
With whispers soft, the nighttime brings.
In quiet realms, reflections roam,
Among the shadows, I am home.

The world falls away, a fading hue,
In whispered thoughts, my essence grew.
Connected in ways, unseen yet clear,
In shadows of one, I hold you near.

With every heartbeat, the night aligns,
In stillness found, our spirit shines.
A dance of souls, entwined, yet free,
In shadows of one, we cease to be.

Diary of a Dreamer

Upon the pages, ink takes flight,
In tender breath of morning light.
A dreamer's heart, so wild and true,
In every line, a world anew.

In swirling thoughts, where wishes dwell,
I capture whispers, weave my spell.
Each fleeting thought, a story spun,
In the diary, my soul's begun.

Night wears a cloak of starlit gleam,
In every shadow, a fleeting dream.
With pen in hand, I chase the skies,
In realms of wonder, a spirit flies.

A tapestry of hope I weave,
In fragile words, I choose to believe.
Through pages worn, my heart will soar,
In the diary of dreams, forevermore.

Altars of the Unseen

In shadows deep, the whispers dwell,
Crafted dreams that never tell.
Veils of night, they softly weave,
Silent stories that deceive.

Beneath the stars, the secrets lie,
With fervent hopes, we dare to try.
Hands raised high, in reverence true,
We seek the light that once we knew.

In corners quiet, magic swirls,
Invisible threads in cosmic twirls.
Each breath held tight, a sacred vow,
To find the grace within the now.

Oh, altars built from dreams and fears,
In every heart, the echo nears.
Where visions dance, and spirits sing,
We honor all that love can bring.

Pilgrim of the Quiet Road

With weary feet, the path unfolds,
Stories lost, and tales retold.
Each step whispers of the past,
With heavy heart, the die is cast.

In the stillness, solace found,
Every echo, a sacred sound.
The gentle breeze, a guiding hand,
Leading through this quiet land.

Stars above like lanterns bright,
Illumining the darkened night.
With every stride, the soul takes flight,
Towards a destiny of light.

Oh, pilgrim brave, do not despair,
For every journey holds a prayer.
In silence flows a sacred stream,
Awakening the deepest dream.

Timeless Whispers

In the hush of dawn's embrace,
Echoes linger, dreams retrace.
Time dissolves, a fleeting sigh,
Where moments pause, and spirits fly.

With every breath, the past ignites,
Flickering flames in starry nights.
Secrets woven in the air,
Whispers soft beyond compare.

Infinity wraps its arms around,
In the silence, truth is found.
Wisdom flows like rivers wide,
Carving paths where dreams abide.

Oh, timeless song upon the breeze,
Cradled gently among the trees.
In the heart, the echoes ring,
Revealing all that memories bring.

The Space Between Words

In quiet gaps, the meaning lies,
Hidden truths that seldom rise.
Silence speaks in subtle tones,
Crafting worlds with heartfelt moans.

The pause between a laugh and tear,
Holds the weight of every fear.
Between the lines, a story waits,
In tender glances, love creates.

Walls that whisper, bridges bend,
In every start, there lies an end.
With every breath, the soul's caress,
In the stillness, we are blessed.

Oh, cherish now the silent space,
Where thoughts converge, and hearts embrace.
In the void, a dance unfolds,
A tapestry of lives retold.

Dancing with Echoes

In shadows deep, where whispers play,
Footsteps linger, they drift away.
The night wind carries a silent sway,
Dancing softly, the echoes stay.

Stars above, they twinkle bright,
Guiding dreams through the endless night.
Each heartbeat feels like pure delight,
In this world, all wrongs seem right.

Among the trees, a melody sings,
Nature joins in, as laughter springs.
Lost in rhythm, the heart takes wings,
Embracing all that silence brings.

With every echo, the spirit soars,
Entwined in peace, forevermore.
In the dance of light, the heart explores,
Dancing with echoes, it's never a chore.

Melancholy's Embrace

Beneath the weight of a heavy sky,
Shadows creep where memories lie.
Lost in thoughts, I quietly sigh,
Melancholy whispers, time drifts by.

Each tear that falls, a story told,
Fragments of warmth in the winter's cold.
In the silence, a heart of gold,
Embracing softness, a world unfolds.

Rivers of dreams, they quietly flow,
Carving the past, where the soft winds blow.
In every heartbeat, the shadows grow,
Melancholy's touch begins to show.

Yet through the gloom, a light shall gleam,
A flicker of hope in the turning stream.
In every sorrow, a promise beams,
In melancholy's embrace, we dream.

Solitary Footprints

Along the shore, where waters kiss,
Footprints linger in gentle bliss.
Each step echoes a soul's deep wish,
Marked by the tides, a fleeting miss.

The sun sets low, painting skies gold,
Stories of wanderers, brave and bold.
In solitude's arms, we break the mold,
With footprints shared, our hearts unfold.

Waves crash softly, a rhythmic song,
Guiding the lost, where they belong.
In every journey, we grow strong,
Solitary paths, yet we feel the throng.

As dawn arrives, the world awake,
Each footprint left, a choice to make.
Stories of lives, in silence stake,
In solitary footprints, destinies wake.

The Heir of Isolation

In a castle high, where winds do howl,
Lies an heir beneath a shadowed cowl.
Silent rooms, where echoes scowl,
Isolation wraps with a spectral towel.

Whispers of dreams drift through the night,
Bathed in moonlight, they take to flight.
In the depth of darkness, visions ignite,
The heir awaits, ready for the fight.

Pages of history, worn and torn,
Each tale lingered, yet souls are sworn.
In the grip of silence, truth is born,
The heir of isolation, never forlorn.

But from the shadows, a voice will rise,
Breaking the chains, revealing ties.
In solitude's arms, hope never dies,
The heir of isolation learns to fly.

The Solitary Path

Beneath the whispering trees, I tread,
Silence wraps around like a thread.
Footprints linger in the soft earth,
A journey marked since my birth.

The wind carries tales of old,
Secrets in shadows, waiting to unfold.
Each step echoes, a heartbeat near,
In solitude's bond, I hold what I hear.

Light dances through branches high,
Painting the ground where lost dreams lie.
Paths diverge, choices to choose,
In quiet moments, I cannot lose.

The horizon beckons, a meandering line,
With every step, I feel divine.
Solitude sings a sweet refrain,
On this solitary path, I remain.

In the Company of Thoughts

Night descends with a gentle sigh,
Stars awaken in the vast sky.
My mind wanders, a restless friend,
In the dark, it seems to blend.

Whispers of memories drift and sway,
Carrying echoes from yesterday.
In silence, laughter, in stillness, tears,
A tapestry woven from hopes and fears.

Each thought a pebble in a stream,
Flowing softly, like a dream.
Companions true, they dance and play,
Guiding my heart, lighting the way.

Alone yet not, I sit with grace,
Finding solace in this space.
The company I keep, a cherished lot,
In the embrace of my thoughts, I'm caught.

The Unwritten Ballad

A song of sorrow drifts in the air,
Untold stories, a world laid bare.
Notes of joy and hues of pain,
Together they form a sweet refrain.

Each heartbeat a rhythm, a secret tune,
Under the watchful gaze of the moon.
Fingers poised, but silence reigns,
In the void, creativity strains.

The quill awaits, in shadows, it hides,
Among the dreams where longing abides.
A ballad unwritten, fierce and free,
Yearning for lips to sing, to be.

In every pause, a tale takes flight,
Starlit whispers bright in the night.
Each line unwritten, a chance to start,
A melody waiting, a song from the heart.

A Canvas of Forgotten Dreams

Brush strokes dance on a weathered sheet,
Colors blend where night and day meet.
Echoes of visions, lost in time,
Waiting for voices to lend them rhyme.

In corners dark, shadows play,
Faded hues from yesterday.
Nebulous thoughts, like clouds, they drift,
Searching for hearts, a silent gift.

Each canvas speaks, a soul laid bare,
Stories of longing, whispers in air.
Textures of hope, woven with fears,
Captured moments, through laughter and tears.

The artist's heart beats soft and slow,
In this world where dreams can grow.
On this canvas, let life expand,
A tapestry crafted by life's gentle hand.

The Path Less Followed

A winding road through misty glades,
Where whispers dance with fading shades.
Footsteps soft on untrod earth,
Each turn reveals a new rebirth.

With shadows deep and sunlight rare,
The path unfolds with gentle care.
Here, silence speaks a heartfelt song,
In solitude, we find where we belong.

Birch trees sway with stories old,
In hidden nooks, the brave and bold.
The journey shapes the soul's embrace,
In stillness, we discover grace.

To choose the road the others shun,
Is to find solace in the run.
Each step a brush with mystery,
In nature's arms, we roam so free.

A Diary of Isolation

Pages filled with ink and sighs,
Revealing truths that time denies.
In quiet rooms where shadows play,
Thoughts unravel, drift away.

A cup of tea, steam rising slow,
Companionship of dreams that flow.
Echoes linger in the night,
A heart alone, a flickering light.

The ticking clock, a faithful friend,
Each moment stretches, hard to bend.
Loneliness wraps a dense cocoon,
While crickets sing a solemn tune.

Yet in this space, a spark ignites,
A deeper understanding lights.
In solitude, we learn to cope,
Finding strength within our hope.

The Stillness Between Breaths

In moments still, where time holds sway,
A gentle pause before the day.
The world retreats, the mind lets go,
In hushed embrace, the spirit glows.

Each breath a wave upon the shore,
In flowing tides, we seek for more.
The silence speaks in whispers soft,
In sacred space, our hearts lift aloft.

In between the notes, a song,
Where everything feels right, not wrong.
The stillness weaves through flesh and bone,
A peace that echoes, felt alone.

To breathe and simply be this way,
Transforms the night, illuminates the day.
In quiet moments, truth is found,
A dance of life, a holy ground.

The Echo Chamber of the Heart

Within the chambers, echoes ring,
The whispers of the love we bring.
Each heartbeat thrums a sacred sound,
In this vast space, we are unbound.

Reflections dance in dim-lit halls,
Resonance in these painted walls.
Fears and dreams collide in grace,
A symphony that time can't chase.

Through laughter bright and tears that flow,
The heart's own rhythm starts to grow.
Carving paths through stone and clay,
This echo chamber finds its way.

In every pulse, a truth revealed,
A canvas of what was concealed.
So let the echoes sing their part,
In this chamber we call the heart.

The Unheard Lullaby

In the quiet of the night, soft whispers play,
Stars twinkle gently, lighting the way.
Moonbeams dance on leaves, a silent tune,
Embracing dreams beneath the pale moon.

Crickets chirp their song, a melody sweet,
Nature's lullaby, where hearts feel complete.
Each breath a whisper, a promise to keep,
As worlds drift away into the deep sleep.

Time slows down in the hush of the air,
Cradled in comfort, free from all care.
The night wraps its arms around weary souls,
In the unheard lullaby, the spirit unfolds.

So close your eyes, let the silence arise,
With each passing moment, find peace in the skies.
In whispers of night, let your heart take flight,
Embracing the calm of the starry night.

Remnants of a Silent Voice

Glimmers of echoes in shadows remain,
Fleeting thoughts linger, a soft, sweet pain.
Words unspoken weave through the air,
Carrying stories no longer laid bare.

In the depths of the heart, a whisper exists,
Yearning for freedom, lost in the mist.
Memories dance like leaves in the breeze,
Haunting the silence with fragile pleas.

Each sigh is a tale, a story untold,
In the quiet of night, their beauty unfolds.
The silence holds secrets, a sacred embrace,
Remnants of voices lost in time and space.

When dawn breaks the clouds, the light starts to creep,
Awakening shadows from their slumbering sleep.
Yet still in the silence, their presence remains,
The remnants of voices, the echoes of names.

Portrait of a Solitary Spirit

In twilight's glow, a figure stands still,
Bathed in soft shadows, a heart full of will.
Brushstrokes of silence paint the night's scene,
A portrait of solitude, quiet sheen.

Wandering pathways with no end in sight,
Each step a whisper, a dance with the night.
A spirit in search of a place to belong,
Finding strength in the silence, deep and strong.

The stars overhead, companions so dear,
Guiding the heart through the darkness and fear.
Each moment a treasure, a gift from the skies,
In solitude's embrace, the spirit will rise.

A treasure of stillness, a canvas so wide,
With colors of dreams where the heart can confide.
In the portrait of solitude, freedom is found,
A serene celebration in silence profound.

The Stillness Tapestry

Threads of the night weave a fabric so fine,
Stitched with the whispers of time's gentle line.
Each stitch a promise, a moment embraced,
In the stillness tapestried, life is encased.

Stars quilt the heavens in shimmering grace,
A tapestry woven with love's warm embrace.
In silence we gather, our hearts intertwined,
Creating a masterpiece, beautifully designed.

Ripples of calm flow through every seam,
Whispering secrets, entwining a dream.
The stillness around us, a canvas so vast,
In this tapestry, echoes of the past.

Let the stillness cradle your hopes and fears,
In the fabric of life, find joy in the tears.
For in every thread, a story unfolds,
The stillness tapestry, a treasure of gold.

Labyrinth of Thought

In corridors of quiet mind,
Ideas twist and turn unkind.
A flicker here, a shadow there,
Lost within a maze laid bare.

Each question leads to another chase,
Through riddles wrapped in time and space.
A flickering flame, a whispered light,
Guides me softly through the night.

Yet in the dark, a seed still grows,
Hope's gentle touch, a bloom that shows.
Within confusion, clarity found,
A sense of peace, profound, unbound.

The labyrinth shifts but I remain,
With every turn, I shed my pain.
Through winding paths, I come to see,
The truth was always inside me.

The Hidden Wilderness

Beyond the roads, where shadows play,
A world awaits, far from the fray.
Ancient trees in silence stand,
Guardians of this secret land.

A canopy where sunlight weaves,
Through tangled vines and whispering leaves.
Creatures shy, with silent grace,
Dance among the wild embrace.

Footsteps soft on mossy floor,
Nature's heartbeat at the core.
Here I find what's lost in haste,
A treasure trove of time embraced.

In wandering paths, serenity,
Each moment is a gentle plea.
To listen close, to learn, to roam,
A hidden place that feels like home.

Solace in the Silence

In the hush between each sound,
A sanctuary can be found.
Where thoughts are few and hearts can mend,
In stillness, sorrows gently blend.

The world outside may roar and cry,
Yet here, the spirit learns to fly.
Amidst the quiet, peace unfolds,
A soothing balm for weary souls.

Each breath a wave, a calming tide,
With every pause, the noise subsides.
In solitude, I come to know,
The strength within, a steady glow.

Embracing calm, I find my way,
In silence, hope begins to sway.
A whisper echoes deep inside,
In solace, I no longer hide.

Archive of Untold Stories

In dusty shelves, the tales reside,
Of laughter, love, and hope, they bide.
Whispers linger in the air,
Each spine a truth, a secret dare.

The ink of lives once lived, now still,
Echoes of passion, dreams to fulfill.
A tapestry of timeless grace,
Each page a glimpse of human place.

Stories yearning to be unfurled,
Of quiet strength and vibrant worlds.
Through every word, a heartbeat fierce,
In silent moments, they will pierce.

With open hearts, we weave anew,
Collecting threads of every hue.
In every tale, we find our part,
An archive stitched within the heart.

Milton Keynes UK
Ingram Content Group UK Ltd.
UKHW022117251124
451529UK00012B/571

9 789916 907337